Everyone Knows Gato Pinto

EVERYONE KNOWS
Gato Pinto
MORE TALES FROM
SPANISH NEW MEXICO

RETOLD BY **JOE HAYES**
Illustrations & Design by Lucy Jelinek

A Mariposa Book

Published by
Mariposa Publishing
922 Baca Street
Santa Fe, New Mexico 87501
(505) 988-5582

FIRST EDITION 1992

Selections from "The Day It Snowed Tortillas,"
"Coyote &," "The Checker Playing Hound Dog,"
"A Heart Full of Turquoise," and "Everyone
Knows Gato Pinto" by Joe Hayes
available on cassette tapes from
Trails West Publishing, P.O. Box 8619,
Santa Fe, New Mexico, 87504-8619.

ISBN 0 933553-09-9

For my wife
Danita Ross

TABLE OF CONTENTS

If I Were An Eagle

*H*ERE IS A STORY ABOUT A POOR ORPHAN BOY. He had no family at all — no father or mother, no sister or brother, not even any cousins.

In order to survive, the boy began to work as a blacksmith's assistant. But the blacksmith worked him very hard and paid him very little. So one day when the blacksmith was away from the forge, the boy made himself a long knife out of steel. He sharpened the knife until it could cut through oaken wood as if it were cheese, and then he set out into the world with the knife in his belt.

The boy hadn't traveled far when he thought he heard voices arguing up ahead of him. He rounded a bend in the road to see a lion, an eagle and a tiny ant shouting at the top of their voices and making angry gestures at one another. Near them lay a dead deer.

"*Animalitos*," the boy called out, "what can be making you so angry?"

"This deer belongs to me," the eagle cried. "I spotted it from high in the air and began to chase it."

The lion interrupted him. "But you were able to do nothing to it. I ran it down and caught it. The deer is mine."

The ant chirped, "It's mine! It's mine! See. It's lying on top of my house. It's mine!"

The boy drew his sharp knife. "I can settle this argument," he told the animals.

First, the boy cut the soft flesh away from the deer's bones. He gave it to the eagle. "You have no teeth," he said to the eagle. "You can eat this soft meat."

Next, he gave the lion the big bones with meat clinging to them. "With your teeth and strong jaws you can gnaw these bones and crack them open. That will give you plenty to eat."

Finally he gave the small bones to the ant. "You are tiny. You can climb inside these bones and find all the food you need."

The animals thanked the boy for solving their problem. Then the lion pulled out one of his claws. "Take this claw," he told the boy. "If you ever find yourself wishing you were a lion, just say, '*Si yo fuera león.*' You'll become a lion."

"Thank you," the boy told the lion. "That will be very helpful. But how do I become a person again?"

"Say, '*Si yo fuera hombre,*'" the lion told him.

Then the eagle pulled a feather from his wing and gave it to the boy. "If you wish to become an eagle, say, 'If I were an eagle.' You'll be an eagle."

The ant pulled one of the tiny feelers from her head. "Just say, '*Si yo fuera hormiga.*' You'll become an ant."

The boy thanked the animals and left them to enjoy their meal. He walked on down the road. Soon he saw a group of evil-looking men riding up the road toward him. Guns and swords bristled from their belts. He knew it was a band of robbers.

At first, the boy thought he'd better turn and run. But if the robbers saw him they could easily chase him down on their horses. Then he remembered the gifts he had received from the animals. He said, "*Si yo fuera hormiga.*" The boy became a tiny ant and the robbers rode right past without even seeing him. When he thought it would be safe, the boy said, "*Si yo fuera hombre.*" He became a person again.

But one of the robbers happened to turn and look back up the road. He saw the boy and gave a shout. They all came charging toward the boy on their horses. Quickly the boy pulled out the eagle feather. "*Si yo fuera águila*," he said and became an eagle. He flew away from the robbers.

Higher and higher the boy flew, farther and farther he traveled, until he saw a castle at the top of a mountain. The castle belonged to a giant, and the giant had a princess imprisoned there.

The boy circled down and landed on the castle wall. He saw the princess sitting in the garden, weaving a cloth with threads of gold and silver. Under a tree nearby, the giant lay asleep.

The boy flew down and perched on a low branch of the tree. When the princess looked up and saw him she said, "Oh, Giant, look at the beautiful eagle on the branch just above you. Catch it for me."

"Let me sleep," the giant grumbled, "What do you want with that bird?"

"I want to put it in a cage," the princess said. "It will be my companion. After all, if you're going to keep me here forever, the least you can do is let me have a pet."

"Foolish girl," the giant growled. But he caught the eagle and put it in a cage. All day long the princess kept the cage hanging beside her as she worked on her weaving. She talked to the eagle and told it how sad and lonely she was in the giant's castle.

That evening the princess carried the cage into her room in the castle and set it near the window. The giant closed the door and locked it, and the princess lay down to sleep. The boy thought, "Now is the time to come out of this cage." He said, "*Si yo fuera hormiga*," and became an ant. He ran between the bars of the cage and down to the floor. "Now I'll show the princess who I really am," he thought. He said, "*Si yo fuera hombre*," and returned to his own shape.

The boy shook the princess's bed and she opened her eyes. The princess was startled when she saw him and cried out. The boy heard heavy footsteps as the giant came running down the hall toward the princess's room. "*Si yo fuera hormiga*," he said quickly. He scurried back up the wall and into the cage. "*Si yo fuera águila*," he said, and put his head under his wing and pretended to be asleep.

"Why did you cry out?" the giant asked as he opened the door.

The princess had seen the boy turn into an ant, and then an eagle. She knew he must be a friend. So she made up a story to tell the giant. "I was just drifting away to sleep, and a terrible dream came to me," she said. "I dreamed that my father's armies came and killed you. I cried out in my dream and woke myself up."

The giant laughed. "Your father's armies will never harm me," he boasted. "No one can hurt me."

"Of course not," the princess said. "You're so strong. Nothing in the world can hurt you. What is the secret of your strength, Giant?"

The giant's chest swelled with pride. "The secret of my power is simple. But the world is full of fools, and they'll never discover it. It is hidden inside a little speckled egg. And the egg is inside a white dove. The dove is in the belly of a black bear that lives in a green valley far away." The giant roared with laughter. "All anyone would have to do is throw that egg against my forehead. Then my strength would be like a natural man's."

"But no one will ever learn that secret, will they, Giant?" the princess said.

The giant roared, "Never!" And walked laughing back to his own room.

But the boy had heard everything. The next day when his cage was hung on the tree in the garden and the giant had fallen asleep in the shade, the boy said, "*Si yo fuera hormiga.*" He ran out of the cage and up onto the branch. "*Si yo fuera águila,*" he said. He flew up over the castle wall.

"Oh, no!" cried the princess. "My eagle has escaped!" But the giant didn't even open his eyes.

The boy flew and flew until his wings were so tired he could hardly move them. Finally, he spotted a green valley in the distance. As he flew over the valley he saw a great

black bear rambling through the trees and thickets. It looked as though no people lived in the green valley, but in the next valley to the east, the boy saw a small house.

The boy landed not far from the house. He said, "*Si yo fuera hombre.*" Then he walked to the house and asked if he could have lodging for the night. The people who lived in the house were kind and told him he could sleep in their stable. They invited him to sit and eat with them.

As they ate, the boy asked how they managed to make a living in that valley, and the people told him, "We have a flock of sheep."

"Who takes the sheep to pasture?" the boy asked.

"Our daughter takes them out each morning, and returns with them at the end of the day."

"Tomorrow I'll take your sheep out to graze, to repay you for your kindness."

The man said that would be fine, but he warned the boy not to take the sheep into the green valley to the west. "A fierce bear lives in that valley. We don't dare enter there."

The next morning, the boy drove the sheep from their pen and started up the valley. When he returned that evening the sheep looked fat and contented, but the boy appeared to be exhausted. He ate only a few bites of supper and then stumbled to the stable to sleep. But he told the people he would tend their sheep again the next day.

The woman said to her husband, "Where can the boy have taken our sheep that they came home looking so healthy? And what do you suppose has made him so tired?"

"Who knows?" the man replied. And then he told their daughter, "Follow the boy tomorrow and see where he goes and what he does."

So the next morning, as the boy drove the sheep across the valley, the girl followed him. She saw that when he was just out of sight of the house he turned the flock to the west and drove them into the forbidden valley.

While she watched from behind a bush she saw the sheep settle down to graze happily on the lush grass. Then the girl saw the black bear rush out of the thicket and run toward the flock. The boy suddenly became a lion and ran to meet the bear's charge. All day long the bear and the lion fought, until finally they fell to the ground beside each other, too tired to move.

Then the bear turned his head toward the lion and said, "If only I had a slab of ice to roll on, I would rise up and tear you into a thousand pieces."

And the lion replied, "If only I had a sip of sweet wine to drink, and a kiss from a pretty girl, I would rise up and tear you into two thousand pieces."

Finally, the bear struggled back into the bushes and the lion became the boy once again. He started home with the flock.

That night, the girl told her parents what she had seen and heard. Her father told her, "Follow the boy again tomorrow. Take along a cup and a flask of sweet wine."

The next morning the girl followed the boy into the valley again. Soon the bear appeared, and the boy became a lion. All day they fought until they fell exhausted to the ground.

"If only I had a slab of ice to roll on," the bear growled, "I would rise up and tear you into a thousand pieces."

"If only I had a sip of sweet wine, and a kiss from a pretty girl, " said the lion, "I would rise up and tear you into two thousand pieces."

The girl ran from behind the bush. She filled a cup with wine and held the lion's head in her lap while he sipped. Then she bent down and kissed him.

The lion rose up, and lashed out at the bear with his paw. The bear's belly split wide open, and a white dove burst out and flew away.

Instantly the lion became an eagle and flew after the dove. When the eagle caught the dove, an egg fell from it and landed in the girl's lap. She held the egg up high, and the eagle swooped down and snatched it from her hand and then flew away.

The boy flew back toward the giant's castle. He arrived the next morning, and saw the princess weaving in the garden. As usual, the giant was sleeping under the tree. The boy flew down and perched on a branch.

"Giant, look!" the princess said, "My eagle has come back."

"Don't bother me," the giant muttered. "Can't you see I'm sleeping?"

So the boy flew down to the ground. "*Si yo fuera hombre*," he said. Then the boy handed the egg to the princess. She ran to the giant and threw it against his forehead.

The giant jumped to his feet, but already he had begun to grow smaller. His hair was turning grey and his skin began to wrinkle. He became a little old man.

The boy took the keys from the giant's belt and set the princess free. She wanted him to return with her to her father's palace, but the boy had other plans.

He flew back to the valley where the kindly people kept their sheep. He married the girl who had helped him overcome the fierce bear. They lived happily together for many years, and he never became a lion or an eagle or an ant again — except when he was an old, old man, and then he did it just to make his grandchildren laugh.

What Am I Thinking?

*T*HERE WAS ONCE A VERY GOOD PRIEST WHO served at the church in a poor village. He was a small man and so everyone just called him Padre Chiquito. The people loved Padre Chiquito for his kindness and wisdom and for his gift of making people feel at peace with themselves.

There was another man in the village who was loved by everyone, but for a different reason. He could make the people laugh. There wasn't a hair on that man's head, so everyone called him Pelón, the bald one. His bald head was full of songs and verses, and especially riddles. He could come up with a riddle about almost anything, but no one else could ever ask a riddle that would stump Pelón.

Pelón was the one who swept out the church and kept the building in good repair for Padre Chiquito. And when the worries of the poor villagers weighed too heavily on the good priest, Pelón managed to keep Padre Chiquito smiling with his jokes and riddles.

One Sunday, just as Padre Chiquito was about to begin the Mass, a carriage pulled up in front of the church, and who should step down but the governor of the province. The governor was a very greedy and cruel man, and there was no telling what trouble he might bring to the village.

The governor strode to the front row of the church and took a seat, and the Mass began. As soon as Padre Chiquito began speaking, the people were calmed. He gave the most beautiful sermon they had ever heard. Their hearts filled with pride in their good priest. And so, when it was time for the collection, the people dug deep into their pockets and brought out every last penny they could afford.

The governor watched this, and thought, "Look at these people. When my tax collectors come around they say, 'We're poor farmers. We have nothing to offer.' But here they are giving their money with both hands to this priest!" And the governor began plotting how he could get rid of the priest.

When the Mass had ended and the people had returned peacefully to their homes, the governor approached Padre Chiquito, shaking his head in concern. "I don't know, Padre," he said. "I'm not at all sure you are wise enough to serve the people of this village. I'm going to give you a test. I will give you three questions, and three days in which to answer them. If you can come to my palace three days from today with the correct answers, you may stay here in this village. But if you fail, I will have you removed and I'll put in your place a priest of my choosing."

Padre Chiquito had no choice but to agree. So the governor looked about him, trying to come up with a hard question. Under a tree on the other side of the street he saw a dog turn around several times in the grass and then lie down.

"This is the first question," said the governor. "¿Cuántas vueltas da un perro antes de acostarse?"

The priest repeated the question to himself, "How many circles does a dog make before it lies down?" How could he give one answer to that question. It would probably be a different number each time the dog lay down.

The governor saw the worried look come over the priest's face, and he smiled to himself. He had already thought of the next question. Here is the second question," he continued. "*¿Qué tan hondo es el mar?*"

"How deep is the sea?" thought Padre Chiquito. "How should I know that? I'm a priest, not a man of science."

The governor smiled broadly. His third question was the best of all. He asked the priest, "*¿Qué estoy pensando?*"

The priest shuddered within himself as he repeated the question, "What am I thinking?" That was an impossible question to answer!

Then the governor turned on his heel and walked out of the church, leaving Padre Chiquito in despair over the difficulty of answering those questions in three lifetimes, let alone three days.

A short while later, when Pelón arrived to sweep out the church, he saw how worried the priest looked. When he learned the reason, he said, "Don't worry, Padre Chiquito. Lend me one of your robes and your little burro to ride to the governor's palace. I'll go and answer those questions for you."

Padre Chiquito didn't really think anyone could answer the questions, but he saw no better solution, so three days later Pelón dressed himself in one of the priest's robes and pulled the hood up over his head. He mounted the priest's burro and went trotting off to the governor's palace.

The governor had invited all his rich friends to watch him make a fool of the good priest. Pelón entered the hall and stood humbly before the crowd. "Are you ready,

Padre?" asked the Governor. Pelón nodded his head. Then the governor stated his first question, "*¿Cuántas vueltas da un perro antes de acostarse?*"

"How many circles does a dog make before it lies down?" repeated Pelón. "That's obvious, Your Excellency. *Todas las que le dé su gana.* As many as he wants to."

The governor's rich friends declared that was a good answer. But the governor wasn't impressed. He knew that was the easiest question of all.

He stated his second question. "*¿Qué tan hondo es el mar?*"

"How deep is the sea?" Pelón said smiling. "*Un tirón de una piedra.*"

"One stone's throw?" laughed the governor. "That's all?" But then he realized the answer was right. If you throw a stone into the sea, it goes exactly to the bottom and no farther. The rich friends nodded to one another in approval.

Well, thought the governor. This priest is more clever than I expected. But still he felt confident. He had one more question, one that was impossible to answer. "*¿Qué estoy pensando?*"

"What are you thinking, Your Excellency? That's the easiest question of all. You think I'm Padre Chiquito, but I'm not. I'm Pelón, the priest's helper!" And he threw back the hood and showed everyone his bald head.

Everyone laughed with delight. And the governor had to swallow his pride and join in the laughter himself. He invited Pelón to stay and eat with him and his friends, and then sent the faithful servant home with the news that Padre Chiquito could stay and serve the good people of the village for the rest of his life. And that is exactly what he did.

How To Grow
Boiled Beans

*T*HIS IS A STORY ABOUT TWO FRIENDS WHO grew up together in the same village. When they were grown, one of them married and stayed in the village, making the best life he could by farming and doing any sort of work that was available. The other left the village to travel around and try his luck in the larger world. He ended up wandering far away. The two friends didn't see one another for many years.

And then one year at the village fiesta, the friend who had stayed at home met up with the one who had gone traveling. The old friends shook hands. "It's so good to see you," said the villager. "Come home with me. Spend the night with me and my family."

So the two friends went home to spend the evening talking about old times. In the morning the friend from far away said he had to meet a man about some business. "But I'll be back soon," he said. He dug his hand into his pocket and brought out two coins. "Here. Take these two pesos. Go and buy a dozen eggs. Ask your wife to fry them for our breakfast. When I return we'll all eat together."

So while the one friend went off to his meeting the other hurried to the market to buy eggs. His wife fried them and they set the table and waited for the friend to return.

When an hour had passed and the friend still hadn't appeared, the man said to his wife, "We may as well just eat these eggs ourselves. My old friend must have forgotten to come back."

"But your friend paid for the eggs," his wife said. "They're not really ours."

"I know what I'll do," said the husband. "As soon as we finish eating I'll go and buy another dozen eggs."

He did that. But they didn't cook the eggs. Instead, the man put them in the nest of one of his own hens so that she could hatch them. "I'll keep track of everything that comes from these eggs," the man said, "and if I ever see my old friend again, I'll share it with him."

The dozen eggs produced eleven young hens and one rooster. In a year's time the hens were all laying eggs of their own and hatching out more babies. The man sold all the eggs he could, and then began selling the chickens as well.

With the money he made he bought a cow, and the cow had two calfs. They grew and had young of their own. He sold some of the cattle and bought sheep. Then with the money he made from selling cattle and sheep he bought land.

He became one of the wealthiest men in those parts. But he always told everyone, "Part of this belongs to my old friend. It all comes from my friend's dozen eggs. If I ever see him again I'll divide it with him."

At the village fiesta ten years later, the friends met again. As before, they shook hands, and the man who had stayed home invited his friend to spend the night. They went to the big house where the villager now lived. It stood in the middle of fertile green fields. Beyond the fields, sheep and cattle were grazing.

"Do you remember the two coins you gave me to buy eggs that morning ten years ago?" the one friend asked the other. "All this comes from that dozen eggs." And he explained just what had happened. "And now," he told his friend, "I want to divide everything with you. Half of all this is yours!"

But the friend from far away said, "No. You're mistaken. If all this comes from the two pesos I gave you to buy eggs, it all belongs to me. I won't settle for anything less."

"But that isn't fair," said the other. "I have worked hard all these years. I've invested your dozen eggs wisely. I've managed the growth of our business carefully. I'll keep half of everything."

"I say it's all mine," said the traveler, "And if you won't give it to me of your own free will, I'll take the matter to court."

Of course the hard working friend wasn't willing to give everything away, so the other man went looking for a lawyer. He had no trouble finding one. In fact, he found two. They both saw a lot of profit for themselves in the case.

As for the unhappy friend who had worked so diligently all those years, no one wanted to defend him. Every lawyer he talked to was on his friend's side. A date was set for the matter to be placed before the judge.

The day before he would have to go alone to the court, the hard working friend sat in front of his house with his head bowed down, lost in his sorrow. An old Indian man from the neighboring pueblo came walking past.

"Amigo," the old Indian said, "why are you so sad? Has sickness come to your family?"

The man shook his head.

"Did somebody die?" the old Indian asked.

Again the man shook his head.

"Then, what is it? It can't be all that bad. You must have a good life, with all this land and this big house. What can be making you so sad?"

Then the sad friend told the Indian the whole story of how he had acquired everything because of the dozen eggs his friend had never returned to eat, and how he was about to lose it all. "I can't even find a lawyer who will present my side of the case," he told the man.

"Let me be your lawyer," the old Indian said. "I can win this case for you. How much will you pay me?"

"If you can save me from my old friend's greed," the man said, "I'll pay you a hundred acres of land and a hundred cattle to go with it."

"That's too much," the Indian said. "Just pay me a bushel of corn. I'm too old to take care of a hundred acres of land."

It was agreed. So the next morning the Indian met the landowner in front of the courthouse at nine o'clock. Under his arm the Indian had a pot of cooked beans, and every so often he would take one out and eat it.

When the proceedings began the Indian sat beside his client eating beans and staring off into space. First one lawyer stood up and made a long speech on behalf of the wandering friend. And then the other lawyer spoke. The judge listened carefully, nodding his head as if he agreed with every point they made. The Indian didn't seem to be listening at all.

When the two lawyers had finished, the judge turned to the Indian. "What do you have to say for your client?" he asked.

The old Indian stood up and shuffled slowly to the front of the court. "Let me ask this man something, *tata juez*" he said, pointing at the friend who had moved away. "Tell me, what did you ask your friend to do with the dozen eggs that morning ten years ago?"

"We already know that," the judge said. "He asked him to fry them for breakfast."

The Indian nodded. And then he said to his client. "What did you do with those eggs your friend gave you money to buy?"

The judge was growing impatient. "We know that too. His wife fried them. Do you have anything new to say, or shall I give my decision?"

"Before you do that, *tata juez*," said the Indian, "I want to ask you something. Could you lend me an acre of land to plant some beans?"

With that the judge lost his patience. "What are you talking about?" he roared. "Finish what you have to say about this case so that I can make my decision. Don't be talking nonsense."

The Indian nodded. "I understand," he said. "But I am asking you to lend me an acre of land so that I can plant some of these beans." He pointed at the beans in his pot. "With the beans in this pot I will grow another crop."

The judge pounded his gavel and shouted. "Stop this foolishness, and stick to the point. What does an acre of land have to do with this case? We're not here to talk about planting beans. And furthermore, who ever heard of growing a crop from beans that are already cooked?"

The Indian shrugged his shoulders, "But, *tata juez*," he said, "I thought that if you could believe that my client's wealth grew from a dozen fried eggs, you would believe I could grow a crop from boiled beans."

The judge held his gavel in mid-air. Then he turned to the two lawyers. "Take your client and get out of my court! This honest man owes him nothing but a dozen eggs."

"Did you forget something, *tata juez*?" the old Indian asked.

"Oh, yes," added the judge. "The eggs must be fried!"

The Coyote
Under The Table

*H*ERE IS A STORY ABOUT AN OLD DOG AND a coyote. The dog belonged to a man and woman who lived on a farm at the edge of a village, and for many years he had served his owners well. He had protected their fields and their chickens from wild animals. He had kept thieves away from their house. But now his old legs were so stiff that all he did was lie in the sun beside the door and sleep.

The dog's owners were very poor. They had a hard time just making enough from their tiny farm to feed themselves. And of course it was an expense for them to feed the old dog. Now they had a new baby, which would add to their expenses. So one day, as they were leaving the house to go to the field to work, the woman said to her husband, "Why do we keep this old dog around? He does nothing but sleep all day long."

The husband said, "You're right. We can't afford to keep a dog that doesn't do any work. This Sunday I'll take him to the woods and get rid of him."

31

The old dog heard what they said and decided he would run away from the farm. As soon as his owners had left, he struggled to his feet and walked off into the hills. His head hung down and he sobbed softly to himself as he walked along.

Then, from under a piñon tree, someone called out to him. "*Oye, perro* . . . hey, dog," the voice said, "why do you walk around looking so sad?"

It was the dog's old enemy, the coyote. Over the years they'd had many bitter struggles, with the coyote trying to steal chickens from the farm and the dog determined to keep him away. But now, when the dog heard someone speak to him, he couldn't hold back his tears.

"Aaauuu," he cried. "They're going to kill me!"

The coyote was puzzled. "Why are they going to do that, dog?"

"They say I'm too old. They say I can't work any more."

"Well," said the coyote, "I have noticed that you don't guard the chickens very well these days. That's why I don't steal from your farm anymore. It's no fun if there's no one to chase me. But we can't let them shoot you. I know what we'll do." And the coyote told the dog his plan.

The dog went trotting off toward the field where his owners were working. They had left their baby asleep under a shady bush at the edge of the field, and the dog lay down not far from where the baby slept.

Suddenly, the coyote came running out of the brush. With his teeth he picked up the baby by its blanket and ran off into the trees. The woman screamed and fainted. The man dropped his hoe and came running across the field. And the old dog ran barking and snarling after the coyote.

As soon as he got into the trees, the dog found the baby lying on the ground. The coyote had left her there, just as he'd said he would. The old dog took the baby's blanket in his teeth and carried her back to her father.

"Good dog!" the man said. "You saved our baby's life!" He hugged and patted the dog.

When the woman recovered her senses and heard what had happened, she said, "How could we think of destroying this dog, just because he eats a few pennies worth of scraps each day? He should eat as well as we do."

"You're right," the man replied. "From now on this dog won't eat scraps. He'll sit right up at the table and eat with us."

From that day on they set a place at the table for the dog each evening, and he sat in a chair and ate whatever his owners ate. When neighbors passed by and saw the dog sitting at the table, they would make fun of the farmer. "Whoever heard of letting a dog sit at the supper table?" they would say.

But the man would tell them, "That dog saved our baby from a coyote that had carried her off. As long as he lives, he can eat at the table with us."

Of course the dog enjoyed his new life. And he kept trying to think of a way to repay the coyote. When the time came for his owners to baptize their baby, he saw his chance. When all the people were at the church for the baptism, he went to the hills and found the coyote. He brought the coyote home and hid him under the table.

Soon all the family and friends arrived and they sat down at the table for a big meal. The dog took his place at the table as usual, and whenever some food passed his way, he would slip it under the table to the coyote.

He slipped a whole leg of lamb under the table, and then a big bowl of posole and a stack of tortillas. And then he passed a bottle of wine to the coyote.

The coyote pulled the cork from the bottle and drained the wine in one gulp. *"¡Ay, caray!"* the coyote said. *"Ahora voy a cantar* . . . Now I'm going to sing!"

"Oh, no!" The dog hushed the coyote. He grabbed another bottle of wine and poked it under the table. The coyote gulped it down.

"*¡Ay, qué caray!*" he said. "*Ahora sí voy a cantar* . . . I'm really going to sing!" And he threw his head back and let out a long howling song.

Everyone jumped up from the table in alarm. But the dog went diving under the table, growling and snapping at the coyote. The coyote ran from the house laughing to himself, with the old dog struggling along behind.

When the dog returned, everyone gathered around to hug him. "That wild coyote wasn't satisfied with just try-ing to steal the baby. He had come back to eat us all. And this dog saved us!"

From that day on, no matter where he went in the whole village, the dog sat in a chair and ate at the supper table with the people of the family. And so the old dog lived out the rest of his days as happy as any dog in this world.

The Golden Slippers

*T*HERE WAS ONCE A QUEEN WHO LIVED IN A big house with her only son, the prince. The king had died years before. The queen was extremely fond of her son and gave him everything he wanted.

But the prince didn't ask for much because he was a very good young man. About the only favor he asked was that his mother have her seamstress make a new dress every day. Each morning the prince carried the new dress to the church in a package. He lit a candle in front of the wooden figure of Saint Mary and said a prayer. He would leave the package in front of the statue, and later that morning the old woman who cleaned the church would dress Santa María in her new garment.

In the same village there lived a very poor woman who had just one daughter. Like the queen, the poor woman had no husband. And like the queen she was extremely fond of her child. But while the prince dressed in royal finery, the poor girl had to go about in rags.

One morning when the prince entered the church, he saw the poor girl kneeling before the statue of Saint Mary. Of course, he didn't want to disturb her, so he sat quietly to wait until she had finished her prayers. But he couldn't help hearing what the poor girl was saying.

"Santa María," the poor girl prayed, "every time I come here you're wearing a beautiful new dress. And I'm wearing the same old rags. Please, would you send me just one of your dresses someday, so that I may come to Mass on Sunday looking lovely, like the other girls do?"

After the girl had left, the prince lit a candle and prayed. He left a new dress for the statue, and then hurried home. He said to the queen, "Mother, have your seamstress make the finest dress she is able to. Send it to the poor girl who lives in the town. And have your goldsmith make a pair of golden slippers for her as well."

Of course the queen did as her son wished, and the servants delivered the gifts to the poor girl. "Look!" the girl cried, "my prayers have been answered." And she hugged and kissed her mother.

Then she ran next door to show the neighbor girls what she had received. What she didn't know was that the neighbor girls were greedy, and the sight of the beautiful dress and the golden slippers filled them with envy. They placed a spell on the slippers, so that whoever put them on would fall into a deep, death-like sleep.

The very next Sunday the poor girl put on her new dress to go to the church and thank Saint Mary. She was about to put on a golden slipper, but then she thought, "These slippers will get dirty as I'm walking to church. I'll carry them, and put them on after I get there."

So she carried her slippers to the church. In the corner, right next to the statue of Saint Mary, she sat down and put one slipper on. She yawned and shook her head because she felt so sleepy. She put on the other slipper and fell into a deep sleep. She slept so soundly that she wasn't even breathing.

The priest arrived at the church and found her. "A miracle!" he gasped. "A new statue of the saint has appeared. And how life-like it is in every detail. No human hand could have produced this work of art!"

The priest placed the new statue in a niche beside the old one and announced to the people that they had been blessed with a miracle.

Now each morning the prince lit candles in front of both statues, and for each he brought a fresh dress.

Soon after this, the prince decided it was time to choose a wife. Of course, he did what princes always do when they wish to find a wife. He planned three evenings of dancing at his house and invited everyone from far and near to attend.

Among the girls who arrived from far away were two who had no fine clothes to wear. But they had come anyway, hoping they might be able to borrow some dresses. As soon as they arrived in the town they went to the church to pray for good luck, and they saw the two elegantly-dressed statues.

"Let's just take the dresses from these statues," one of the girls said.

"Of course!" said the other. "The saints won't mind lending us their dresses. Their petticoats are fancier than our dresses anyway. And we'll have the dresses back before morning."

So that evening the two girls attended the dance in the dresses they had borrowed from the statues in the church. They had a wonderful time, even though they didn't seem to attract any special attention from the prince. But, for that matter, neither did any of the other girls at the dance.

The next evening the girls went again to the church to borrow the dresses from the statues. Imagine their delight to discover that the statues wore new dresses!

Once again a fine time was had by all who attended the dance, but the prince still didn't seem to be falling in love with any of the young women.

As the third evening approached, the prince was growing worried. Maybe his plan wasn't going to work after all. So before the hour of the dance, the prince went to the church to light candles in front of the saints he was so devoted to. When he entered the church, what should he see but two young women about to remove the dresses from the statues.

The prince crept up closer to find out what the two girls were up to. He heard one of them say, "These dresses are even more beautiful than the last two. Surely the prince will notice one of us in these dresses."

"I don't know," sighed the other. "I wonder if he'll fall in love with any girl."

And then the first said, "I know what I'm going to do. Look at the golden slippers this statue has on. I'm going to wear them tonight. That will catch the prince's attention!" The girl removed one slipper from the statue.

"Look!" said her friend, "Santa María moved her leg. She must be angry that you're taking her slippers!"

The other girl laughed and said to the statue, "Don't worry, Santa María, you'll have your slippers back before morning." She pulled off the other slipper.

The statue yawned and stretched and rubbed her eyes. "Oh," she said, "what a sleep I've been having!"

The two girls were frightened and ran from the church, but the prince recognized the poor girl. He ran from his hiding place. "Please, go with me to the dance tonight!" he begged her.

They went to the dance together, and, of course, it wasn't long before the two of them were married. They put the golden slippers on the real statue of Saint Mary, and to this day the two of them go each morning to light a candle in front of Santa María and bring her a fresh new dress.

Caught On A Nail

*I*N A LITTLE FARMING VILLAGE HIDDEN IN A mountain valley they tell a funny story about three young men who fell in love with the same girl. The girl wasn't really interested in any of the three, and the young men just about drove her crazy trying to win her attention.

Almost every night at least one of them would stand outside her window and sing love songs to her. Sometimes two of them, or even all three, would show up on the same evening. Then there would be a howling contest to see who could sound loudest and most forlorn. In the daytime, they tried to impress her by racing past her house on fast horses. Whenever she walked on the street one of the young men would hurry to catch up to her and have a conversation, or offer her a flower.

No matter how much the girl ignored those men, or told them right out that she didn't like them, they wouldn't leave her alone. Finally she came up with a plan to teach them a lesson.

First she went to a carpenter in the village. "How much do you charge to make a coffin?" she asked the carpenter. When he told her the price, she said she would pay him twice that amount if he would make a coffin with-out telling anyone about it and haul the coffin to an empty house that stood at the edge of the village. Everyone claimed the house was haunted. They said strange lights were seen in that house.

The next time one of the young men spoke to her on the street, she told him to go to the old house at eleven-thirty that night. "There is a coffin in that house," she told him. "You'll see a candle burning at the head of the coffin. If you are brave enough to lie in the coffin all night long with a cloth over your face like a dead man, I just might become interested in you."

The young man was delighted that she had finally taken notice of him, and he swore he could do just as she told him.

Later that day the second of the young men tried to speak to her and she told him to go to the same house at fifteen minutes before midnight. "You'll find a coffin in that house, and there is a dead man in it. If you are brave enough to pull a chair up next to the coffin and pray over the dead man all night long, I just might talk to you from time to time."

The second young man was delighted too. He said he wasn't the least bit afraid to do as she asked.

Later, when she met up with the third young man, she told him to go to the house right at midnight. "Inside the house there is a dead man in a coffin, with another ghost in a chair beside it saying prayers. If you are brave enough to dress up like the devil — with your face all blacked with charcoal and cow horns tied to your head — and dance around those dead men all night long, I might be able to enjoy the pleasure of your company."

Of course the third young man said he would do it.

42

A little before eleven-thirty that night the girl went to the house. The coffin was there, just as the carpenter had promised. She lit a candle at the head of the coffin, and then hid in a back room to see what would happen.

Sure enough, at eleven-thirty, the first young man arrived at the house. He saw the empty coffin with a candle burning at its head. The girl saw him shudder as he climbed into the coffin and pulled a cloth over his face. Then he lay perfectly still.

Fifteen minutes later the second young man arrived. He dragged an old chair over near the coffin and began to pray in a quivering voice. The rosary beads rattled in his fingers.

Suddenly, just at midnight, the young man in the chair looked up and saw the devil come dancing through the door. "¡Ay, Dios mío, el diablo!" he shouted.

The first young man jumped up out of the coffin. "You're not going to get me yet!" he hollered and went diving out a window.

When the young man in the devil suit saw the dead man jump up out of his coffin, he spun around and ran right back out the door. Down the road they went, the dead man hollering at the top of his voice, "No! No!" with the devil right behind him.

But the other young man didn't even get up out of his chair. He just kept praying louder than ever. The girl couldn't help but be impressed. She came out of her hiding place and said to the young man, "You really are brave. You didn't run away."

The young man turned his white face toward her. "*¿Y cómo quieres que corra?*" he asked. "How do you expect me to run? *Se me engancharon los pantalones en un clavo.* My pants are stuck on a nail."

And just then the nail popped out of the chair. The young man fell to the floor face first and then jumped up and ran down the road after the other two.

The next day the girl told everyone in the village what had happened, and the young men were so embarrassed, they never bothered her again.

And to this day, in that village when someone has done something that seems to have taken a lot of courage and brags about it, people will say to him, "Maybe you're brave. Or maybe your pants just got caught on a nail."

The Man Who Couldn't Stop Dancing

*T*HERE WAS ONCE A MAN WHO OWNED A HERD of goats. But he was too busy to tend the goats himself. He thought he would go to the village and hire a boy. He found a boy who had no father and lived alone with his poor mother. The boy was anxious to work so that he could help her. So he accepted the man's offer to pay him four pesos a week. He traveled back to the man's ranch with him.

The boy turned out to be a good goatherd. He soon knew all the goats by name and they would come when he called. He could milk the goats quickly, and got more milk from them than they had ever produced before. But it was a hard life for the boy and he was often hungry and sad.

One morning as he was driving the goats into the mountains to eat grass, the boy met an old woman along the way. He greeted her politely, *"Buenos días le dé Dios."*

"Buenos días. What are you doing here, *nietecito?"* the old woman asked him.

"As you can see, *abuelita*," the boy replied, "I'm taking care of these goats."

"I see," said the old woman. "And is it a good life, taking care of goats?"

"I have no reason to complain," the boy said. "But I do get a little hungry sometimes."

"Take this," the old woman said, and handed him a folded cloth. "Every time you unfold this cloth there will be something good to eat inside."

The boy thanked the old woman. 'It's nothing," she told him. "Is there anything else you need?"

"Well, I do feel a little sad and lonely sometimes."

"Then take this," the old woman said. From under her cape she brought out a little violin. "Play this. The music will make you happy."

"But I don't know how to play," the boy told her.

The old woman laughed. "You can play this violin. It's a magic violin. And do you see this little white key here at the end? If you turn that key, before you play, everyone who hears the music will have to dance."

Again the boy thanked the old woman, but she just waved her hand and walked on down the road.

When the boy arrived at some good grazing land the goats began to eat, and he sat in the shade of a tree to rest. He put the violin under his chin and drew the bow across the strings. He was amazed at the sweet music that came out. He sat for hours playing the violin while the goats grazed peacefully.

About midday he began to grow hungry. All his master's wife had sent along for him to eat was a bit of dry bread. The boy thought, "The old woman told me the truth about the violin. It really is magical. I'll unfold the cloth and see if she told me the truth about it too."

When he unfolded the cloth the boy saw the most delicious meal he could imagine in front of him — bread and meat and cheese and fresh fruit of all kinds. It was much more than he could eat. He ate what he could and then set the rest aside carefully. He folded the cloth again, and closed his eyes and took a nap.

The boy woke up with a start. The goats were making frightened noises, and so he looked about to see what the problem was. Two coyotes were creeping toward one of the youngest goats. The boy grabbed a big rock to throw at the coyotes. And then he thought of something else. He picked up the violin and turned the little white key at the end.

The boy drew the bow across the strings and a lively tune sprang from the violin. The goats all looked away from the coyotes. They stopped making frightened noises. Instead, they stood up on their hind feet and began to dance. And the coyotes did the same thing!

The boy played on and the goats danced more and more wildly. And the coyotes' dance was the wildest of all. The boy played until his arm was so tired he couldn't go

on. When he quit playing the goats all fell to the ground exhausted. And the coyotes rolled over onto their backs and fell asleep. When they woke up, they felt so happy, they didn't even think of bothering the goats. They went away wagging their tails.

That evening when the boy arrived home with the goats, they looked healthier than ever before. And they gave twice the amount of milk they had been giving. Of course the boy's master was pleased. But he was also a little suspicious.

The master's wife was suspicious as well when the boy seemed to have no interest in the bread and thin soup she served him for his supper.

Every day the boy took his cloth and violin and drove the goats back to the mountains. He spent the days playing music and eating good food. When wild animals came to bother the goats, he turned the white key on his violin and made all the animals dance. Each day the goats were more content and gave more milk. And each day the owner and his wife grew more suspicious.

Finally one day the master decided to follow the boy to the mountains and find out what was going on. He arrived at the pasture just about noontime and watched the boy and the goats from behind a bush. He saw the boy playing his violin softly and the goats grazing peacefully.

Then the master saw the boy set down his violin and unfold his cloth. The master had never seen such a meal! His mouth began to water. So that was why the boy never ate his supper any more!

The master hurried away to tell his wife what he had seen. His wife told him, "Go to town and buy a piece of cloth like the one you saw the boy unfold. Tonight while the boy's asleep we'll take his cloth and leave the new one in its place."

So the man rushed off to the store and bought a cloth that looked just like the boy's. That night he crept into the stable where the boy slept and took his cloth.

The next day the boy was very disappointed when he unfolded his cloth and no food appeared. But he said to himself, "Oh, well. Nothing can last forever. At least my violin still works." And he chased away the empty feeling in his stomach with the music of his violin.

But when he got home that evening and saw that the master and his wife were just finishing a big meal (in fact, they looked as though they'd been eating all day), the boy knew what had happened.

After he had milked the goats and settled them for the night, the boy took his violin to the master's house. "Master," he said, "I noticed that you and your wife just finished a very good meal. Would you like me to play you some music? It might help you digest your food."

The master had heard the sweet music the boy made with the violin, and he thought this would be a perfect end to the trick he and his wife had played. They had stuffed themselves on the food from the boy's cloth, and now they'd let the boy lull them to sleep with the music of his violin. "Oh yes, boy," the man said. "Play us a song."

The boy reached up and turned the little white key on his violin and then began to play. Right away the man's feet began to tap. His wife began moving about in her chair.

"Play a little slower," the master said. "I don't seem to be able to sit still when you play like that."

But the boy didn't play slower. He pulled the bow

faster and faster across the strings. The master and his wife were dancing around the room, kicking their feet over their heads. "Stop! Stop!" they cried. "That's enough music." But the music only grew wilder. Soon they were banging against the walls and falling over the furniture. They begged and pleaded with the boy to stop his music.

"Give me back my cloth and I'll stop," the boy told them.

"It's under the bread box in the kitchen!" his mistress cried.

The boy went into the kitchen and found his cloth. Finally he stopped playing. The man and woman lay on the floor, too tired and bruised to move or say a word.

"Pay me the money you owe me," the boy told his master. "I don't want to work for someone who steals from me."

"Pay you money?" the master roared. "I'll have you thrown in jail!"

The first thing the next morning, the master went to the village to bring charges against the boy for beating him and his wife. He told the *aguacil*, "You'd better bring along some helpers. That boy is dangerous."

When the sheriff and two helpers arrived at the ranch the boy was playing a quiet tune on his violin. The sheriff told him, "Boy, you must come with me. Your master has charged you with beating him and his wife."

"Of course I'll go with you," the boy said. "Just let me finish playing this song."

"No!" cried the master. But it was too late. The boy reached up and turned the little white key on his violin.

Soon the sheriff and his assistants were dancing a-round the yard. They hit their heads on branches of trees and fell into ditches. "Stop!" they begged, "Stop! We'll let you go in peace."

"Tell my master to pay me the money he owes me," the boy said.

"I'll pay! I'll pay!" the man shouted. He struggled to get his hand into his pocket. He pulled out all the money he had and threw it at the boy. "Take all of it. Just stop your music!"

The boy stopped playing and picked up the money, and while all the men sat panting for their breath and rubbing their bruises, he walked away.

He went back home and gave the money to his mother. And then he unfolded the cloth and while his mother ate her fill of all the delicious food, he played her a gentle tune on his little violin.

Gato Pinto
(The Spotted Cat)

ONCE THERE WERE THREE GROWN BROTHERS who lived with their father in the same house, which was really just one big room. Their mother had died many years earlier.

When the father died, the sons took his will to have it read. They found out that their father had divided the house among them. He left a certain number of vigas, or roof beams, to each.

The oldest son was willed six vigas. The part of the house that lay under that much of the roof would belong to him. So at the sixth beam from one end of the house the oldest son built a wall and made a spacious room for himself.

The second son received four vigas from his father. He used the wall his older brother had built for one side of his room. Four beams farther along he built another wall. His room was smaller, but still quite comfortable.

The youngest son, whose name was Juan, received just the last two vigas at the end of the house. That wouldn't make much of a room for him. But Juan was a cheerful young man and he didn't complain. He just shrugged his shoulders and said, "Oh, well. At least I don't have to build a wall to turn my end of the house into a room. My brother's wall will be on one side, and the outside wall of the house will be on the other."

Juan began living in the narrow room under just two ceiling beams at the end of the house. But his older brothers were very spiteful, and they envied even the two beams their younger brother had received. One of them said to the other, "Our father's will said that two vigas should go to our foolish little brother Juan, but it doesn't say anything about the latillas that are laid across the beams to make a roof. Let's take them and use them for firewood."

And they did that. Now Juan had two beams over his head, with nothing but the sky for a roof. On cold nights he would build a fire on the floor in the middle of his room to keep warm. When he went to bed, he would spread the warm ashes on the floor and sleep on top of them. He was always covered with ashes, and his brothers started calling him Juan Cenizas.

One night a stray cat jumped over the wall of Juan's room and moved in with him. It was a white cat with black and brown spots, and Juan named it Gato Pinto. Juan was happy to have the company and shared bits of his tortillas with Gato Pinto. At night he always spread a little extra patch of ashes for the cat to sleep on. During the day, everywhere Juan went, the cat went with him. Everyone who knew Juan knew Gato Pinto.

Then one evening Gato Pinto began digging in one corner of Juan's room. The constant scratching annoyed Juan, so he picked up the cat and carried it back to the middle of the room. But Gato Pinto returned to the corner and continued to dig. Again Juan carried the cat away, but it returned to the corner. Juan was growing angry and was about to throw the cat outside when he noticed that Gato Pinto had dug up a little wooden box. He opened the box and found a paper inside.

The next day Juan went to an old friend of his father's to get help reading the paper. "This paper was written by your father," the friend told him. "It says there is another box buried below the one you found."

"Does it say what's in the box?" Juan asked.

"Oh, yes. The box is full of money. Your father wanted the money to be for you alone."

Juan hurried home and dug deeper in the corner. He found another wooden box, and when he opened it, he saw more money than he had ever seen in his life. The friend had to help him count it. Then the friend told him, "Juan, if you stay here, your brothers will find out you have all this money, and they will try to take it away from you. You'd better leave this place."

"Oh, no," said Juan. 'I don't think my brothers will do that." He was going to return home, but Gato Pinto picked up the sack full of money in his teeth and ran away.

Juan ran after him, but couldn't catch up. All day long he followed the cat. When night overtook him, Juan built a fire and camped under a big tree. He could see Gato Pinto creeping around the edge of the circle of light made by his fire, but the cat wouldn't come close to him.

Juan was awakened in the morning by a rooster crowing and saw that he was near a town. Gato Pinto ran to the edge of the town with the sack of money, and then dropped it. Juan thought, "Maybe our old friend was right. Maybe I should live in this town."

Juan bought a house in the new town and settled down. His brothers never knew what had happened to him, but they really didn't care. Many years passed. And then the brothers began to hear about a rich man named Juan who lived in the neighboring village. People said this Juan was very kindhearted and good to all the poor people of the village. And they said the rich man had a spotted cat that was always with him. "Everywhere Juan goes," the people said, "the cat goes with him. Everyone knows Gato Pinto."

The brothers asked one another, "Could it be Juan Cenizas? But how could he become rich — unless he stole money that was rightfully ours!"

The brothers decided to find out about this rich man named Juan. They knew of a girl in the market who sold parrots. The brothers visited her and asked, "Do you have a parrot that can ask questions and remember the answers?"

"That one," the girl said, pointing at a big green parrot. "That one can talk like a judge, and it can remember everything it hears."

The brothers paid the girl to offer her parrot for sale in the neighboring village. They told her, "Don't sell it to anyone except the rich man named Juan."

The girl did as she was told, and one day as Juan was walking home from church he saw the girl with her parrot. She looked so poor, and the parrot was so pretty, that Juan bought the bird from her.

That evening, the parrot struck up a conversation with Juan. "*Oye,* Juan," the bird squawked, "don't you have a family?"

Juan answered honestly, "I have two brothers, but I had to leave them because I was afraid they might harm me to get my money."

"Money?" rasped the parrot. "Where did you get money?"

Juan told the parrot the whole story about his cat's discovery. Of course, Gato Pinto was listening. Later, after Juan had gone to sleep, the cat climbed up to the parrot's perch. He grabbed the bird by the throat and gave it such a shaking its brains were rattled and everything it had heard was switched around in its head.

In the middle of the night, when the girl came to question the parrot and find out what it had learned, the bird said, "Aawwk! Juan has two cats. The oldest one got six boxes of money from his brother. Aawk! His father scratched a paper in the corner and found a box full of brothers. Aawk!"

By the next evening the parrot's brains had settled back into place and it struck up the same conversation with Juan. Juan wasn't surprised because he knew parrots will often say the same thing over and over. He told the bird the whole story a second time, and enjoyed talking to the parrot so much, he took the bird into his room with him when he went to sleep. He perched the parrot on the window sill right beside his bed.

Gato Pinto scratched and scratched at the door, but Juan wouldn't let him in. Finally Juan grew so impatient he threw the cat outside. Then, as soon as Juan fell asleep, the parrot flew out the window and back to the girl. He told her all about Juan, and she hurried to tell his brothers. The brothers decided they would set Juan's house on fire that very night while he slept. Since they were his only relatives, they would inherit his money.

But Gato Pinto ran to the village church. He jumped up and sank his claws into the bell rope and began swinging back and forth. The bell rang and rang, and the priest woke up. He came running to find out what was going on.

Of course the priest recognized Juan's cat. Everyone knew Gato Pinto. At first he tried to chase Gato Pinto away, but the cat just climbed higher up the rope. Then the priest thought, "Maybe something has happened to Juan." He ran out of the church and off toward Juan's house. Gato Pinto kept ringing the bell, and soon half the village was awake and running along behind the priest.

The people arrived just in time to see Juan's house beginning to burn. Two men ran away from the house but the people caught them. They put out the fire and woke up Juan.

Juan recognized his two brothers, but he told the crowd, "Let them go. I don't think they'll bother me anymore." And he was right. His brothers were so ashamed of themselves, they never returned to that village again.

And Gato Pinto was never seen around the village again either. No one knew what became of him. Some people said, "That spotted cat was really an angel. It was sent by Juan's father to look after and protect him." And that's what almost everyone in the village began to believe.

As for Juan, he didn't know what to think. But as the years went by, even though he took in many other stray cats, and loved them all, he never found another like his Gato Pinto.

The Little Snake

*T*HERE IS A STORY ABOUT A MAN WHO HAD just one daughter. She was all the family he had in the world. The man worked as a woodcutter, and he and his daughter lived very simply.

One day the girl asked her father to bring home a head of cabbage for her to cook for their supper. Although the woodcutter was very poor, he always tried to please his daughter, so when he returned home that evening, he brought with him a big head of cabbage.

"This big head of cabbage is more than we can eat at one meal," the woodcutter told his daughter. "Cut it in half, and we can get two suppers from it."

The girl took the head of cabbage into the kitchen and with a knife cut it in two. And in the very heart of the cabbage she found a little snake. It was shiny and black, with a round head, and it was no bigger than a worm. The girl covered the snake with a cabbage leaf, and then called for her father to bring her a jar to keep it in.

But her father told her, "That animal will hurt you some day. *Vale más que lo mates.* You'd better kill it right now."

"*Papá!*" the girl exclaimed. "How could I kill this snake? It's going to be my best friend."

So her father brought her a jar. She fed the snake each day and held it in her hand and talked to it. The snake grew so fast that in a week's time she had to ask her father for a larger jar.

Again her father warned her, "That animal will hurt you some day. *Vale más que lo mates.* You'd better kill it right now."

And again she answered, "How could I kill this snake? It's going to be my best friend."

Her father brought her a larger jar and she put her snake in it. She continued to feed and care for her snake and every week she asked her father for a bigger and bigger jar. Finally she asked her father for a barrel for her snake.

For the final time her father told her, "That animal will hurt you some day. *Vale más que lo mates.*"

"How could I kill this snake? It's my best friend," the girl said.

The woodcutter brought his daughter a great round barrel to keep her snake in. Each day she would take her snake out of the barrel and spend hours talking to it. It told her many wonderful things. It told her that whenever she cried, she made rain fall from the sky. Whenever she laughed, she made pale blue and pink and white flowers grow. And when she sang, bright red and orange and yellow flowers grew. The girl's happiest hours were the ones she spent talking to the snake.

But the snake continued to grow, and one day when she returned it to the barrel, the girl saw that it could no longer live in so small a space. That night the snake told the girl that it would have to leave her. She wanted to go too, but the snake said it wasn't possible. She begged and pleaded, and finally the snake said, "This is the best I can do for you. Follow my track in the morning. When you arrive at the end of the trail, make a wish for what you need most. You shall receive it."

In the morning the girl ran to the barrel and saw that the snake was gone. From her window she could see its trail leading away from the house, and she followed the trail. It led her far away, to lands she had never even heard of before. And then the trail began to grow faint. In the middle of a barren plain, the trail disappeared.

The girl looked all around her and saw nothing but the most desolate country she could imagine. Not a green tree or bush grew in that land. The girl thought of her father and their comfortable little house, and she sat on the ground and covered her face with her hands and began to cry.

From the clear blue sky above her a gentle rain began to fall. It was just as the snake had told her! The thought made her laugh. Pale flowers grew up all around her — blue and pink and white flowers. A song sprang from her lips, and bright flowers grew at her feet.

"I wish I had a good house to live in, right here on this spot," the girl said aloud. And the wish was granted. A snug little house stood behind her.

The girl began living in the house. Whenever she felt happy and sang or laughed, flowers grew around the house. When she missed her father and cried, rain fell to feed the flowers. Soon the house sat in the center of a beautiful garden with flowers and fruit trees of all sorts.

But the garden was in the middle of a country that was dry and dying. No one could grow anything. No one could find grass for their livestock to eat, nor water for them to drink. Not even the king himself could coax a green sprout from the fields that surrounded his palace.

Now, the king owned a flock of sheep. They had once been fat, healthy animals, but they had grown so thin and weak that the king feared they would all die. One day he told his shepherd, "Take my sheep and drive them to the far mountains. There is nothing for them to eat here, and in the mountains some grass may still be growing."

So the shepherd drove the sheep away from the king's lands. He hadn't traveled a third of the way to the mountains when he saw a little house standing in the middle of a rich garden. No matter how hard he tried, he couldn't keep the sheep from running to the garden and eating. He was afraid the owner of the garden would be angry, but the girl who lived in the house just smiled to see the sheep eating so greedily. At the end of the day, she even gave the shepherd a basket of fruit to take home with him.

When the shepherd returned to the king's palace that evening, the king was amazed to see how fat and contented his sheep looked. He was even more amazed to see the basket of fruit.

"Where does this fruit come from?" he asked the shepherd. "And where did you find green food for my sheep to eat?"

The shepherd told the king about the house in the middle of a garden of fruit and flowers, and about the gentle girl who lived in it. "I must meet this girl," the king said. "Go tomorrow and invite her to have dinner with me."

The next day the shepherd returned to the garden and invited the girl to dine with the king. But the girl replied, "If the king would like me to visit him, let him come himself and invite me."

The following day the king himself rode to the girl's house and invited her to join him for dinner. She traveled back with him to the palace, and that evening as they ate,

64

the king asked her to tell him the story of her life. As the story unfolded a look of wonder came over the king's face. Finally he jumped up from the table and said, "Wait! I must show you something."

The king ran from the room, and when he returned he brought with him a shiny black snake skin. He explained to her that many years before, when he was hunting in the mountains, he strayed into the garden of an evil magician. He had tasted a leaf from a head of cabbage in the garden and fallen under a spell.

"I don't remember anything that happened for what must have been years," the king said. "And then one morning I woke up in the desert, not far from my palace, with this snake skin beside me."

"Then you are my best friend!" the girl cried. And it was true. And not long after that he became her husband as well. They left the palace and its barren fields and moved into her house in the middle of the fertile green garden.

But the girl always wondered what had become of her father, so they journeyed back to her old home. They found the woodcutter looking very old and very sad, from long years of thinking about how his beloved daughter had disappeared. When he saw her, he was finally able to die in peace.

The girl returned with her husband to live among the flowers and trees of her garden. And whenever the thought of her father brought a tear to her eye, rain fell to make the garden grow even greener.

The Magic Ring

*T*HIS STORY IS ABOUT THE RICHEST AND MOST powerful king in the world. Because he was so rich and powerful, he didn't have enough worries on his mind and was always coming up with ridiculous ideas.

This rich and powerful king had no children, and one day the queen said to him, "Husband, even though you are the richest and most powerful man in the world, you won't live forever. Who will be king after you are gone?"

The king decided that he would think of a way to find a proper successor to the throne. "I know what I'll do!" he said to his wife. "I'll issue a proclamation. I'll say I want to find the strongest man in the land. I'll have a contest. Any man can come and compete. And the one who proves himself to be strongest will be the next king."

"But what if the people don't like the strongest man in the land?" the queen asked. "Or what if he turns out to be foolish or cruel?"

But the king just waved his hand and said, "The king has spoken!" And so the word was sent throughout the country, and strong men from all over came to the palace to try their strength and demonstrate their skill.

In a faraway corner of the country a young shepherd heard about the king's proclamation. The boy wasn't even the strongest man in his own village, but he said to himself, "What if I should turn out to be the strongest man in the land? What if I should become the next king? What a life I could have then!"

He began thinking about it all day long as he watched over the sheep, and he dreamed about it all night long as he slept next to his flock. Finally he told his mother what was on his mind. She said, "Don't be silly. Why would you want to waste your time with the king and his contests? If he had any sense, he wouldn't be holding such a contest in the first place."

But the boy kept insisting that he would like to try his luck, and finally his mother gave him her blessing. "But before you leave," she told him, "go and visit our neighbor. You know she's a sorceress. Maybe she can help you in some way."

So before he left for the palace, the shepherd visited their neighbor. "I'm going to the king's palace to see if I can prove to be the strongest man in the land," he told her. "Do you have anything that can help me?"

The old sorceress opened a trunk and dug down to the bottom. She pulled out a little gold ring, and told him to wear it on his right hand. She said that every time he blessed himself with the sign of the cross, his strength would double. If he made the sign of the cross backwards, his strength would be cut in half.

The shepherd boy thanked his neighbor and hurried off toward the king's palace. As he walked along, he saw a wagonload of hay sitting outside a house by the side of the road. He thought he would find out if the sorceress had told him the truth.

He walked over to the wagon and tried to lift a wheel off the ground. It didn't budge. He put the ring on his right hand and then blessed himself. "*En nombre del Padre y del Hijo y del Espíritu Santo.*" Now he should be twice as strong. When he tried to lift the wheel it moved slightly from the ground.

The shepherd blessed himself again. Since he was already twice as strong as usual, he should now be four times as strong. He lifted the wheel clear to his waist.

Again he blessed himself. He should have eight times his normal strength! The wagon tipped over when he lifted it with one hand, and hay scattered all over the ground!

The young man hurried to set the wagon upright and reload the hay before the owner noticed what he had done. He made the sign of the cross backwards to reduce his strength before it got him into trouble. He took off the ring and put it in his pocket, and then went on his way.

That night the shepherd slept under a tree beside the road. And in the night, the ring fell from his pocket. The next morning he woke up and stretched, and then traveled on toward the king's palace, leaving the ring on the ground under the tree.

Later that morning, a priest came traveling along on his donkey. He was making his rounds from village to village. He stopped to rest under the tree, and he saw something shiny on the ground. "Oh, a ring!" he said. "That must be worth something. I'll just wear it until I get to the next town, and then sell it and give the money to the church."

The priest rested in the shade for a while, and then before resuming his journey, he knelt to say a prayer. He blessed himself, "*En nombre del Padre y del Hijo y del*

Espíritu Santo," and then began to pray. He didn't know
that he was twice as strong.

When he finished his prayer, he blessed himself again.
He was four times as strong. As he rose from his knees, he
reached out and grabbed a branch to steady himself. He
tore the branch from the tree. "Oh!" he said to himself,
"That looked like a solid branch, but it must have been
rotten." He gave the branch a toss and it flew out of sight
across the field.

The priest shrugged his shoulders and walked over to
where his little burro was eating grass. "Well, little friend,"
he said, "we'd better be on our way." He patted the burro's
neck, and the poor animal was knocked to the ground. Its
neck was almost broken.

The priest gasped, "Heaven help us! What is going on here?" And he blessed himself again. Now he was eight times as strong! He took hold of the burro's saddle and pulled, to help it back to its feet. The little beast flew ten feet into the air. "What?" said the priest. And the strength of his voice blew all the leaves off the tree.

"This place is bewitched," the priest thought, and he hurried on down the road, praying and blessing himself as he walked along.

In the meantime, the shepherd had reached a village. When he put his hand into his pocket for a coin to buy a bite to eat, he noticed that his ring was gone. He started back to find it. Soon he saw someone coming toward him, knocking down trees, pulling up fences and raising a great cloud of dust.

The priest saw the shepherd boy and tried to warn him. "DON'T COME NEAR ME," he whispered with a voice like the bellow of a bull. "JUST THE SOUND OF MY VOICE MIGHT HURT YOU!"

The shepherd stopped and called out, "Father, did you find a ring?"

"YES!" whispered the priest.

"Bless yourself backwards, Father," the young man told him. "Your strength will return to normal."

The priest began to make the sign of the cross backwards. Each time he did it, his voice grew softer, and his feet stirred up less dust when he moved. Finally he thought his strength was reduced to normal, and he said to the shepherd, "Here, take your ring back. I want no part of it." He threw the ring to the boy.

But the priest was still twice as strong as normal, and the ring shot right past the boy. It landed in the tall grass beside the road about a hundred yards beyond him. "That's all right, Father," the shepherd said. "I'll find the ring. Go on. The people will be waiting for you at the church."

The priest went on, and the shepherd stayed to look for his ring. But he couldn't find it. He walked up and down parting the grass. He crawled on his hands and knees. The ring was too well hidden. Finally the shepherd boy decided he would go into the village for something to eat and then return to search some more.

He had hardly left, when a little old woman came walking up the road, leaning on her cane. She was on her way to church, praying softly to herself as she walked along. She saw the ring in the grass beside the road and picked it up. She slipped it on her finger.

Before long she blessed herself, "*En nombre del Padre y del Hijo y del Espíritu Santo*." She reached up to take out the handkerchief she had stuffed into her sleeve, and tore the sleeve off her dress. "*¡Válgame Dios!*" she said. "How did that happen?"

Soon she blessed herself again, and then again. She came upon two men who were trying to move a stubborn mule. One man was tugging on the reins in front of the mule and the other was pushing from behind, but the mule had its hooves dug in and wouldn't move.

"Shame on you, you stubborn old mule," the old woman said to the animal. "Stop being so lazy." And she nudged the mule with her cane. The mule flew past the man in front. It didn't touch the ground until it was fifty feet beyond him. It hit the ground running and disappeared down the road.

The old woman went back to her praying. By the time she reached the church, she was so strong she pulled the door from its hinges. As she walked up the aisle, she knocked over benches and sent people rolling onto the floor.

The priest looked up from his book. Before he even saw the ring on her finger, he knew what had happened. "*Señora*," he told her, "make the sign of the cross backwards."

She obeyed him, and her strength grew less and less. When she had only the strength of a young woman left, he told her to stop. Then he sent someone to find the shepherd and tell him to come for his ring.

The shepherd put the ring on his finger, and didn't take it off again. Finally he arrived at the king's palace.

The courtyard was full of strong men showing off their muscles. They uprooted trees and threw great boulders over houses. They wrestled with one another and fought with swords. Finally one of them, a handsome prince in fine clothes, defeated all the others. The king declared that the strongest man had been found. "If there is anyone else who wishes to challenge the prince," called out the king, "let him say so now."

The shepherd stepped forward. "Your majesty," he said, "maybe I could be stronger than the prince." Everyone turned to look at the ragged shepherd. He wasn't especially tall. His shoulders weren't very broad. His legs were long and thin.

The king frowned. "You can't challenge the prince," he said. "You don't even own a decent suit of clothes."

But the shepherd said, "Your majesty, your proclamation said that anyone could enter the contest. I want to challenge the prince."

So the king said that in one week the prince and the shepherd would compete to see who was stronger.

The king ordered his craftsmen to make four great pillars — one of wood, one of stone, one of iron and one of gold. He said that anyone who could lift a pillar of each

73

material would surely be the strongest man in the world.

All week long the prince trained for the contest. He lifted big rocks over his head and wrestled with ten men at a time. The shepherd slept all day long in the hay in the king's barn. When the week had passed, a crowd gathered to watch the prince and the young shepherd compete.

First the king led them to the pillar of wood. "Which of you can lift this?" he asked.

The prince huffed and puffed and stretched and twisted, and then wrapped his arms around the pillar. He lifted it from the ground. A cheer went up from the crowd.

The shepherd blessed himself, "*En nombre del Padre y del Hijo y del Espíritu Santo.*" And then he blessed himself again for good measure. He placed a hand on either side of the pillar and then threw it into the air. It rose until it was just a tiny speck in the sky. When it fell to earth, it shook the windows in the king's palace.

The king was very surprised, and the prince began to look worried. Next they walked to the pillar of stone. For a long time the prince stretched and groaned and then wrapped his arms around the pillar. He lifted it a few feet from the ground, and then dropped it. Again the crowd cheered.

The shepherd blessed himself again. He threw the pillar over his shoulder. Into the air it sailed. When it hit the ground, a crack appeared in the wall of the king's palace.

The king led the prince and the shepherd to the pillar of steel. The prince threw all his strength into the task. He lifted the pillar an inch or so from the ground.

The boy blessed himself, "*En nombre del Padre y del Hijo y del Espíritu Santo.*" He launched the pillar into the air. When it landed, the ground shook with such force that the palace cracked in two.

Finally, the king conducted them to the pillar of gold, but the prince had used up all his strength, and couldn't even try. The king said to the shepherd, "If you lift the pillar of gold you will be king after I die, and in the meantime, the pillar of gold will be yours. You may keep it!"

But the shepherd said, "No. I don't think so. Just look at all the harm your foolish idea has done. Who knows? If I become the king, I might end up as foolish as you. I think I'll just go home."

The boy set out for home, and when he got there, he blessed himself backwards until his strength was just what it should be. Then he gave the ring back to the wise old woman.

And what happened at the palace? Well, the queen sat the king down and told him, "It doesn't matter if that shepherd is stronger than the prince or not. It wouldn't matter if he were only half as strong. He's twice as wise as you are, and he should be the next king."

For once the king listened to the queen. And you can probably guess the rest of the story, so there's no need to tell it.

ABOUT THE STORIES

If I Were An Eagle   This tale is extremely common and popular in Hispanic New Mexico. It has frequently been borrowed by Native Americans as well. Variants appear in many collections. A telling similar to mine is in *Spanish Folk-Tales of New Mexico* by José Manuel Espinosa.

What Am I Thinking?   This is a very widespread tale, probably best known in the English ballad "Prince John and the Abbot of Canterbury." A humorous character called El Pelón occurs frequently in Hispanic tales. The corrupt ruler is usually a prince or king, but Adelina Otero made him a governor in her book *Old Spain in Our Southwest*. The change has a ring of historical accuracy. Each colonial governor was required to make an official visit to every settlement upon arriving in New Mexico, which explains why the governor turned up when he did in the story.

How To Grow Boiled Beans*   Stories of a poor, unlettered person who demonstrates great wisdom in settling a dispute are popular around the world and probably reflect the distrust common people often have of legal systems and formal education. The theme is expressed especially well in this tale because Indians were of low social status in Spanish New Mexico. For me the tale also celebrates the value of cultural diversity and the contributions differing groups can make to one another. This tale is adapted from "El indio abogado" (*Cuentos Españoles de Colorado y Nuevo México* #34).

The Coyote Under The Table   This is a popular tale and one that's been told to me on several occasions, although only in summary. It is an old European story even though the Southwestern version features the coyote. There is a German version in the Grimms' tales, and J. Frank Dobie offers a Tex-Mex telling in *The Voice of the Coyote*.

The Golden Slippers*   The tradition of carving *santos* (wooden statues of saints) is as old as the first Spanish colonization of New Mexico. Like the statue in this tale, many *santos* are held in great reverence and some boast quite elaborate wardrobes. The statue of *La Conquistadora* (recently renamed Our Lady of Peace) in the Saint Francis Cathedral in Santa Fe, for example, is said to have some three hundred dresses. This tale is adapted from "Nuestra Señora del rosario" (*Cuentos Españoles de Colorado y Nuevo México* #141).

Caught On A Nail   I collected this brief tale in Peñasco, New Mexico, when working as artist-in-residence at the elementary school. In the original, however, as tape recorded by an uncle of one of the children, the third man was unable to run because he defecated in his pants. (*¿Cómo quieres que corra? Estoy todo cagado.*) Writers and storytellers often "clean stories up" to meet contemporary standards.

The Man Who Couldn't Stop Dancing   This tale is common in many lands. Of course, the magic instrument isn't always a violin. Frequently, the owner of the magic instrument is sentenced to hang and as a last request asks to be allowed to play one final song, but I didn't let things go so far in my telling. A New Mexican variant can be found in *Spanish Folk-Tales of New Mexico* by José Manuel Espinosa. There are two versions in *Cuentos Españoles de Colorado y Nuevo México* as well.

Gato Pinto*   This story is adapted from "Juan Cenizas" (*Cuentos Españoles de Colorado y Nuevo México* #242). It is obviously related to the "Puss In Boots" tale. The division of a house among children by vigas was a common practice in Hispanic New Mexico well into the twentieth century. The appearance of an angel or a departed soul in the form of an animal to help a deserving person occurs frequently in traditional tales.

The Little Snake*   This tale is adapted from "La viborita" (*Cuentos Españoles de Colorado y Nuevo México* #245). A number of tales of a snake, or more often a little worm (gusanito), which is befriended by a girl, grows to enormous proportions and then becomes her benefactor occur in the Hispanic tradition in New Mexico. Cleofas Jaramillo offered another example in her long out of print book *Spanish Fairy Stories*.

The Magic Ring*   What struck my fancy in this tale was the potential for trouble caused by a ring that increases the wearer's strength every time he blesses himself. The priest was in the original, but I added the old woman because I wanted to play with the idea some more. Also, in the original the queen has no role and the king is seeking a husband for his daughter, rather than a successor to the crown. This tale is adapted from "El pastor afortunado" (*Cuentos Españoles de Colorado y Nuevo México* #226).

*Adapted with permission of the Museum of New Mexico Press from *Cuentos Españoles y Nuevo México* by Juan B. Rael, copyright 1977.

THE ILLUSTRATOR

Lucy Jelinek is an artist-designer who has worked in New Mexico since 1978. Her company, Santa Fe Pre-Print, is a graphic design firm specializing in publications. She has designed and illustrated many books by Joe Hayes.

THE PUBLISHER

Mariposa Printing & Publishing was established in 1980. Our goal is to provide quality commercial printing to the Santa Fe community and to provide quality-crafted, limited edition publications in various literary fields.

Your comments and suggestions are appreciated. Contact Joe Mowrey, owner-production manager, Mariposa Printing & Publishing, 922 Baca Street, Santa Fe, NM, 87501. (505) 988-5582